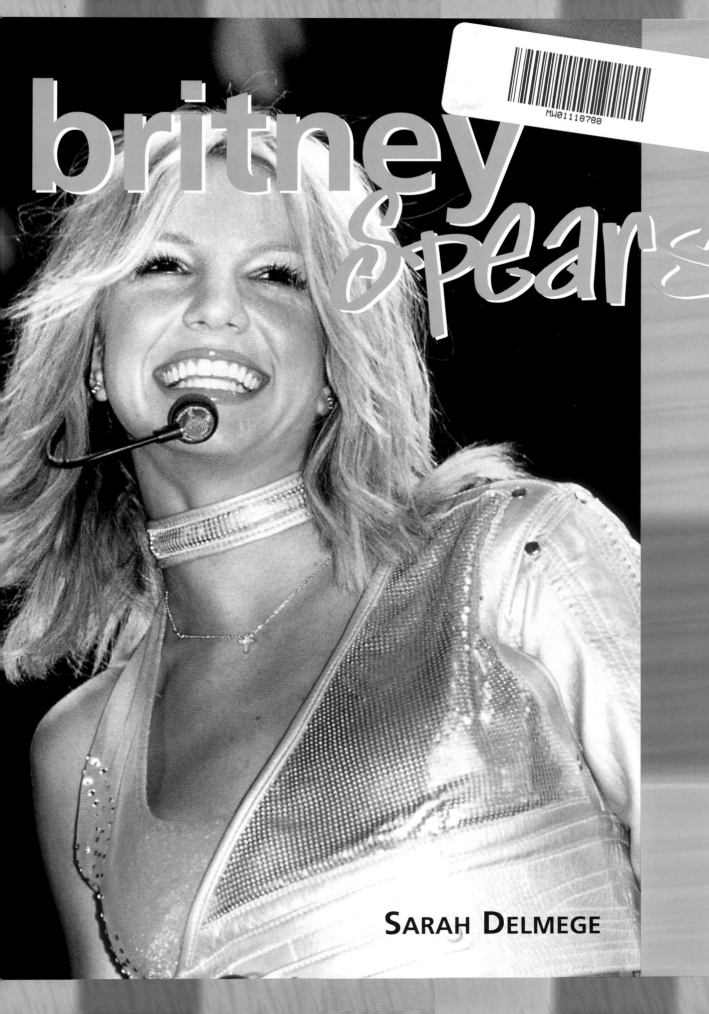

britney *Spears*

SARAH DELMEGE

THIS IS A CARLTON BOOK

Text and Design copyright © 2000, 2001
Carlton Books Limited

Pictures © The publishers would like to thank the
following sources for their kind permission to
reproduce the pictures in this book:

All Action 31/ ©Susan Moore 15
Corbis/ 45 Famous/ Paul Adrian 5l/ Pete Best 4/
Fred Duval 26, 41cl/ Paul Fenton 12/ Sebastiano Pessina 19/
London Features International Ltd.1, 13, 17, 36, 39/
George DeSota 9br/ FGO 32/ David Fisher 3/ Gregg
DeGuire 25, 27, 30, 40, 43/ Marc Larkin 4, 24br/ Jen Lowery
34tr/ Colin Mason 42/ Ilpo Musto 21bl/ Joy E. Scheller 6tr /
Ron Wolfson 2, 16, 20, 22-3, 37
Pictorial Press Ltd. 18, 21tr, 25tl, 33, 38
Retna Pictures Ltd./ © Kevin Estrada 11/ ©Sandra Johnson
7,10, 48/ ©Steve Granitz 5br/ ©Eddie Malluk 9tl /
©Ernie Paniccioli 6l, 8, 14br
Rex Features Ltd./ Brian Rasic 14tl, 41c,cr/
A di Crollalanza 34/ David Hogan 24tl/ Sipa Press/
Jean Catuffe 29/ Mirek Towski 37/ Stuart Cook 46/
Kevin Wisniewski 28

Every effort has been made to acknowledge correctly
and contact the source and/ or copyright holder of each
picture, and Carlton Books Limited apologises for any
unintentional errors or omissions which will be
corrected in future editions of this book.

This edition published by Carlton Books Limited 2001
20 Mortimer Street, London, W1N 3JW

A CIP catalogue for this book is available from the
British Library.

ISBN 1 84222 421 2

Art Editor: Adam Wright
Design: Michael Spender
Picture research: Catherine Costelloe
Production: Garry Lewis

Contents

Introduction

Britney Spears may look like any other normal American teenage girl, but she's living proof that dreams can come true. Her first single, "Baby, One More Time," has gone double platinum, with sales of more than two million, while her debut album has gone triple platinum with more than three million in sales.

Britney is the first new artist—and the youngest ever—to have a debut single and album simultaneously hit the number 1 spot. She's proved to be the biggest thing to hit the music business and the public in years and has rocketed to the top of the charts all over the world. And when you remember that she's only 19 years old, you can tell there's something really special going on here. Something bigger than anyone could ever have imagined.

About the only way, you won't have heard of Britney Spears is if you've been living on a secluded desert island with no radio, TV, papers, or magazines. She's taken the whole world by storm and left it begging for more. Britney fever is everywhere. And it's going to get even madder. There are already Britney wannabes all over the place—the record companies took one look at her success and dollar signs flashed up in their eyes. One or two Britney clones are even experiencing huge success themselves, following in the footsteps of the original princess of pop. But while they may have talent, they will never be Britney Spears. It may have helped that she came armed with some of the most fantastic pop songs ever written, but Britney has made it because of who she is.

Girls can relate to her because she's the kind of girl that could be in your class, the kind of popular girl that everybody wants to be friends with. Britney is a very genuine, down-to-earth girl who happens to be incredibly talented.

But while her fame seems to have come so quickly, she's put an incredible amount of hard work into her success. Even before she became Britney the pop star she'd spent plenty of time working toward her ambition, auditioning for singing, acting, and dancing roles. She's worked hard to make it. So let's celebrate the real Britney Spears story...

The ESSENTIALS

FULL NAME:
Britney Jean Spears

HOMETOWN: Kentwood, Louisiana

ZODIAC SIGN: Sagittarius

CURRENT RESIDENCE: New York and Kentwood

FAMILY: Parents—Jamie and Lynne Spears
Siblings—Bryan and Jamie Lynn

FAVORITE ACTOR:
Tom Cruise, Ben Affleck, Brad Pitt

FAVORITE COLOR: Baby Blue

FAVORITE DRINK: Sprite

FAVORITE SPORT: Basketball, Golf, Tennis

FAVORITE DISNEY CHARACTER: Goofy

FAVORITE STORE: Gap

FAVORITE WAY TO HANG OUT: Shopping at the mall with good friends

HOBBIES: Singing, Dancing, and Reading trashy novels

Favorite Movies: *My Best Friend's Wedding* and *Steel Magnolias*

FAVORITE SPORTS ACTIVITIES: Basketball and Swimming

NATURAL HAIR COLOR:
Blonde

HEIGHT: 5' 5"

BIRTH DATE:
December 2, 1981

FAVORITE FOOD:
Pizza, Ice-cream (cookie dough flavor), Pasta, Hot Dogs

FAVORITE ARTISTS:
Mariah Carey, Madonna, Whitney Houston, Michael Jackson

FAVORITE TEAMS:
Chicago Bulls and New York Yankees

COLLEGE MAJOR HOPEFUL:
Business or Communications

Growing Up

BRITNEY was born the second of three children to a second-grade teacher, Lynne, and a building contractor, Jamie Spears, on December 2, 1981. She was christened Britney Jean Spears and has her mom to thank for the unusual spelling of her first name.

"My mom said everyone spells it Brittany, but that's not how you say it," explains Britney. "And Jean is my mom's mom."

Lynne remembers Britney as a truly sweet and lovable baby who showed signs of her future career almost from the day she was born. The tiny Britney absolutely adored music and was singing before she could talk. And as soon as she could stand she was taking her first wobbly dance steps.

"It drove Mom crazy," Britney laughs. "She told me that even when I was in my cot, I used to like the radio turned up loud."

The young Britney grew up in a cosy, ranch-style house in the heart of the Deep South in Kentwood, Lousiana, or Spears Country as people from her home town like to call it now. It's a small town, with a population of only 2,468, the kind of place where everybody knows everybody and where neighbors would often pop in to say hi, drink coffee, and sample Lynne's famous brownies. Britney had a regular childhood.

I still have the girliest room in the world

She was a girl's girl and loved to be surrounded by girlie things. Her bedroom still looks the same now—she describes it as baby blue with a daybed and lots of dolls. She collects angels and there's hardly a corner in the room without a little cherub smiling serenely out at you!

"I still have the girliest room in the world," Britney laughs. "It's because I haven't really lived there for two years. So it still looks the same. I'm like, eeeeek!"

The Spears are a very close-knit family and Britney realized from a very young age how lucky she was to have such loving parents.

"They make sure I'm OK and safe," she says. "Dad treats me like I'm his baby. He's real sweet and affectionate. But I think I'm more a mama's girl. All my bad habits are from her! Biting my nails and worrying... but she's the most positive person—and that's the quality I want."

Britney adores her older brother, Bryan. Although growing up together they swung between being best friends and worst enemies just like any other brother and sister the world over. Britney remembers one time when Bryan was tickling her and wouldn't stop, so she ended up hitting him over the head with a knife sharpener!

"It broke!" she says, shaking her head disbelievingly at the memory. Luckily Bryan wasn't hurt, only slightly bruised. "He's a hard-headed thing!" she laughs.

Britney's also incredibly close to her baby sister, Jamie Lynn, who's a whole ten years younger than her. Like her big sister, Jamie Lynn loves music and it's formed a close bond between the two of them.

"I like to take care of her. She's really really sweet," Britney reveals. "One time she had my CD in her stereo and was just singing away," she laughs. "She doesn't know any of the words, she was just making them up."

Jamie Lynn reminds the whole family of Britney, or Brit-Brit as she was nicknamed when she was little. She attended a preschool run by her mother, which put her way ahead of the other kids when she went to kindergarten. She was also way ahead of the other kids when it came to her love of music. The little Britney loved to perform and made her singing debut at the tender age of five, crooning "What Child Is This" at her kindergarten graduation. Britney was a hit. Practically the whole town remember her performance to this day.

"I had a balance beam in the middle of the living room floor when I was little for gymnastics," Britney remembers. "And I was always singing and dancing in front of the TV."

And that's something her big brother Bryan remembers only too well...

"She was always performing and belting out these songs," he remembers, laughing. "I'd yell at her to shut up, because I couldn't hear the TV."

Britney persuaded her mom to enroll her at a gym in Covington, an hour's drive from the family home. The little girl shone at the sport and was soon the proud owner of several state titles, which her mom still has on display at home. Britney particularly loved the floor exercises as they allowed her to show off her skill at dancing. She was also incredibly good at the uneven bars.

When I first started doing gymnastics, I loved it so much," remembers Britney. "I'd cry if I missed it

Music took a back seat when gymnastics started to take over more and more of her life. Britney switched to a seven-day-a-week program. The schedule was grueling— the little girl had to practice for three hours every single day. Despite her incredible determination and motivation, it all started to get a bit too much for her.

"I started crying if I went to gymnastics," she admits. "It was over the top."

So Britney decided to take a break and returned to her first love of dancing and, of course, singing. She joined a state competing company and spent most of her free time traveling around the state competing in group and solo dance competitions. Of course, she didn't win everything, but her amazing talent shone through. Even at that age, Britney knew exactly what she did and didn't want to do. Her mom remembers

that Britney would never enter the same competition twice. Showing that even then she had a mind of her own, she'd tell her mother, "Oh Mom, if I did that it would be so tacky."

It was around this time that Britney, who was also singing in church and local talent shows, joined her mom and a friend on a road trip to Atlanta that would change her life. Her mom had heard about an open call audition for the Disney Channel's *New Mickey Mouse Club* and Britney was determined to enter.

"I really wasn't expecting to make the first cut," she says today, "There were so many kids there."

It was certainly a tough competition, with hundreds of kids from all over America wanting their shot at stardom. Britney had never had formal singing lessons, but she was able to copy the sass and style of her idols Madonna and Mariah Carey perfectly. The casting director liked what he saw and to her surprise Britney made it through several auditions. Unfortunately she didn't make it to the end.

My mom was always having these little doubts and everything, because people were like, 'She's what? She's not even a teenager and you're sending her to New York'

The casting director took her to one side and told her that she was too young for the Mouse Club, but he'd been blown away by her talent and suggested her mom take her to New York to get her agent.

After much discussion, her parents decided that Britney was too young for such a big step. So, she returned to the Deep South for more local talent competitions... and boredom.

"I got real antsy," she confesses.

Determined not to give up, Britney carried on competing and when she was nine an audition in Baton Rouge landed her a spot on *Star Search* in Los Angeles. She still has a video of her first TV appearance, which she says she can't watch without laughing.

"There was my big ol' dress and me with a big ol' bow on my head," she remembers giggling. "It looked like I was about to fly away. I said. 'Mama, what were you thinking?'"

It seemed quite obvious that Britney was destined for a showbiz career, so Jamie and Lynne decided to prepare her properly. Soon after Britney made the move to New York for the summer. Together with her mother and Jamie Lynn, who was still only a baby, Britney moved into a sublet apartment in Manhattan's Hell Kitchen. Her brother and father stayed behind in Kentwood. Britney is still incredibly grateful to her parents for allowing her to take such a big step, especially as Jamie and Lynne have often been accused of pushing their daughter into a showbiz career. Britney is determined to set the record straight that it was actually her pushing her parents and not the other way round and that she knows it wasn't an easy decision for her mom and dad.

"My mom was always having these little doubts and everything, because people were like, 'She's what? She's not even a teenager and you're sending her to New York' and all this. But my parents know this is what I wanted to do, and I'm just thankful they were behind me one hundred percent all the time. So it was really me pushing."

Britney studied for three summers at New York's Off Broadway Dance Center and the Professional Performing Arts School. Dance, drama, singing, and every other aspect of performance became her life. Britney loved it. She always had a smile on her face and got on well with her classmates. She got her first real taste of fame when she appeared in several national commercials and starred as an evil child in *Ruthless*, an off-Broadway play based on the movie *The Bad Seed*.

"It was a lot of fun," she says now, looking back on that exciting period of her life.

By the time she turned eleven, Britney had a huge amount of experience under her belt and her raw talent had been honed through her endless dance and performing arts classes. Now it was time to get serious. She decided to try out again for the *New Mickey Mouse Club* and this time she was offered the gig almost straight away. Britney was already making history as the show's youngest performer. She'd started on the path to fame, as had several of her fellow Mouseketeers. *Felicity*'s Keri Russell, 'NSync's Justin Timberlake and JC Chasez, and Christina Aguilera also went on to stardom after appearing in the show. As the little girl of the bunch, Britney might have been forgiven for letting it all go to her head, but amazingly it didn't seem to affect her at all. That wasn't part of her personality and her parents wouldn't have allowed it anyway, but Britney was having way too much fun to even think about it. She found that she fitted in very well with the rest of the crew. With her very girly long brown hair combed with straight bangs, she looked like butter wouldn't melt in her mouth. She was having the time of her life.

"I was pampered because I was the youngest," she says now of her time as a Mouseketeer. "We got to sing, dance, and act so it was an awful lot of fun. We'd walk through the park to get to work. It was really laid back and I had two days off. We filmed for half the year and the other half I would go home. I really had it made and didn't know it." Despite her tender age, she now knew that she wanted to make her career out of music.

On the occasions when Britney was back home, she was in and out of the Parklane Academy, her obliging high school.

Sadly two years later, the show was canceled. Britney and her fellow Mouseketeers had to go their separate ways. For Britney that meant going back to Parklane Academy on a permanent basis—not a thought that really appealed. She spent a year doing what all normal schoolgirls do— playing basketball, attending parties, and hanging out with her friends at the mall. And she tried hard to throw herself back into her old life, though deep down she knew it wasn't for her.

"I did the homecoming thing and the prom thing and I was totally bored," she remembers, sighing.

Although from the outside it seemed as if Britney was settling back into a normal school life, inside she was growing more and more restless. She was frustrated and felt totally out of place at Parklane. Fortunately for Britney, and the rest of the world, it wouldn't be long before she was back on the road to fame.

'Dreams can come True

At 15, Britney got the opportunity to audition for an all-girl singing group—one of the many bands that was springing up in the wake of the huge success of The Spice Girls. Britney enjoyed the experience, but she knew it wasn't for her. She'd never wanted to be part of a group—she had far too much sense of her own direction to be limited by the needs of other people.

One thing the audition had brought home to her, was how much she needed to be performing again. She needed to see what else was out there. So Britney and her parents got on the phone to New York entertainment lawyer Larry Rudolph, whose clients included Ghostface Killah of Wu-Tang Clan. He asked Britney to send him a photograph of herself and a recording of her singing. Larry was impressed and phoned an excited Britney.

"We're like, 'Well is there anything going on?' and he's like, 'No, not really, but you know, pop music is back. I think it would make really good sense for you to come up here and try and get a solo deal.'"

In June 1997, Larry sent a demo tape to Jive Records who liked what they heard so much they immediately set up an audition for Britney. She knew this was her big chance and was understandably nervous at the thought of singing in front of the record company big-wigs. But as soon as she started to sing Whitney Houston's "I Have Nothing," she forgot everything and lost herself in the song. The record company loved her.

"She was a little scared when she first came in," remembers Barry Weiss, the president of Jive Records, "but once she started singing she blew us all away. She became this different person."

They signed her on the spot. At just 15, Britney had achieved her life-long ambition—a record deal. She was over the moon. It seemed too good to be true. Actually, though she couldn't have know it, Jive Records had been looking for someone just like Britney for a while.

Britney fitted Jive Records' requirements exactly. In the wake of the Spice Girls phenomenon, American record companies realized they had very few bands that teenagers wanted and, even more importantly, that teenagers' parents would let them listen to. The record companies knew they had to find a sound that would appeal across the board, unlike rap, swingbeat or Marilyn Manson's goth metal. The music industry was already full to bursting point with girl bands and boy bands. What they needed was a solo performer who could deliver innocent, teen pop with bags of energy, neat dance moves, and just a little bit of sex appeal thrown into the mix. As soon as Britney started singing, Jive Records knew they'd found precisely what they were looking for.

"Britney was unique in that she's a package entertainer: a performer, an actress, a dancer, and a singer," said Kim Kaiman, Jive's director of marketing. "She's very much a symbol of her peers—she's better than that, she's a role model."

Now they'd found their girl, the record company knew they had no time to lose. There was a long hard slog ahead before Britney's career could be launched. It was decided that Britney should go to Sweden to work with the legendary writer and producer Max Martin, one of the hit makers behind The Backstreet Boys and Britney's heroine, Whitney Houston.

Britney spent most of the spring of 1998 recording songs for the album with Max. The two clicked immediately and Britney still credits Max as part of the reason for her enormous success.

He's a genius. He wrote for The Backstreet Boys, for 'NSync, for Ace Of Base. I think his style and his sound is really popular

Together they crafted a sugar-coated sound that's pop yet funky, pure but sassy. It wasn't a quick or easy process. Writing lyrics and setting them to music, not to mention arranging them, took many months. Britney was determined not to produce anything less than perfect. They spent long days and nights shut away in the Cheikron Studios in Stockholm getting every part of the album exactly right. Britney often wished she was outside in the sunshine or actually out there performing her songs, but she knew that this painstakingly long process was crucial if she was going to achieve any kind of lasting success. Vocals were laid down, time and time again, until everybody was happy with them, and

the instrumentals were added layer, by layer until the sound was absolutely perfect. Britney kept a close eye on the lyrics in particular. She didn't mind being a little suggestive, but if anything sounded too adult it was rewritten over and over until it said exactly what she wanted it to.

It's this Britney outlook on life that has singled her out from the rest of her musical peers, such as The Backstreet Boys and 'NSync. Over the past two years, these acts have sold 30 million albums, a stack of top ten singles, and nearly half a billion dollars' worth of merchandise. But they don't have anything approaching the charm of Britney's blossoming character and personality.

Britney and Max came up with an album crammed full of potential hits, including a country-style ballad, "From The

I have guy dancers too— and believe me that helps

Bottom Of My Broken Heart," a Jamaican dancehall-flavored tune, "Soda Pop," also on the soundtrack to TV's *Sabrina The Teenage Witch,* and a remake of Sonny and Cher's "The Beat Goes On."

"I'd never heard of that song," Britney recalls. "I wasn't happy with it until we had a photo-shoot and everyone was older than me and went, 'I love that.'"

Finally it was time to deliver the master tapes to Jive Records. The label had, of course, been keeping a close eye on the recording session. This was only natural, as they were counting on Britney being huge not only throughout America, but hopefully in a number of other countries too. As soon as they heard the album they knew they were on to something good. As the record bigwigs sat down in a conference room and listened to the recordings there was a sense of electricity in the air, the realization that they were all involved at the beginning of something big. But although they knew the music business inside out there was no way they could have imagined the way Britney would explode on to the music scene.

Now the album was complete, it was time for Jive's publicity and promotion machine to crank into gear. For a solo artist wanting to make it big in pop music, publicity was necessary. Britney had to quickly become a familiar face if she was going to be more than a one hit wonder. Jive launched a huge promotional blitz. Britney traveled across the country, appearing at malls. She performed a four-song set with two dancers, before meeting the kids who had come to watch her handing out goody bags filled with samples of her music and some biographical information. Word spread fast and hundreds of kids turned up at every mall to watch this gifted singer who could also dance like a dream. Her polite southern manners soon won over anyone who met her. Britney also appeared on radio shows and the record label set up a World Wide Web page that featured pictures of Britney together with videotaped footage and loads of music clips.

Britney also landed a tour as the opening act for 'NSync, who were just beginning to make it big. It was a gig that any new artist would have killed for, but Britney was especially delighted because it meant being reunited with her old

friends, JC Chasez and Justin Timberlake from the *New Mickey Mouse Club*. She was nervous about meeting them again—after all they were now established music artists—but the moment she met JC and Justin again, it was as if the years apart had never happened and soon they were giggling and chatting like old friends. It was a great chance for Britney to expose her music to an even larger audience, but she knew it wouldn't be easy. The audience had come to see a boy band; how would they react to a girl solo singer? She needn't have worried. Everyone who saw her act fell head over heels in love with the little girl with the huge voice.

"It's been an incredible intense time," Britney told a reporter, "It hasn't always been easy opening for these guys, since there were all girls in the audience. But I ultimately am able to win them over. I have guy dancers too—and believe me, that helps."

Britney loved touring, but not everything always went perfectly. She remembers one performance when she was dancing across the stage and her foot slipped on a cupcake that someone had thrown! She took a nasty spill and landed heavily on her bottom. Her dancers helped her up and, like the true professional she is, Britney carried on with the show. She's also lost her headset on-stage during a song. Then there was the time she tried to disguise a pimple on her face with eyeliner so it would look like a beauty spot. Unfortunately the "beauty spot" ended up looking like a big old mess after her sweaty routine smeared the make-up all over her face! There are bound to be more embarrassments along the line, but Britney has learned that the show must go on no matter what happens—even if her cheeks become a little redder than normal.

Britney
the Super ☆

For someone so young, Britney showed a shrewd understanding of the music business. If anyone in the music business had thought they'd be dealing with an impressionable schoolgirl, they were far wide of the mark. Britney had plenty of ideas of her own.

Maybe she didn't write her own songs (how many great singers do? People praise Elvis and Sinatra but how many words or notes of their material did they actually write?), but she did want control over the way she was marketed. She had ideas and was determined to get them across. She knew she had to establish an identity that set her apart from the dozens of new faces that are constantly being launched by the music industry. She also knew that the biggest music buyers are teenagers, and their tastes change more quickly than street fashion. Britney was more than aware of all that—after all she was still a teenager herself. She was determined right from the very beginning to stay one step ahead.

When she heard Jive's idea for her first video, "Baby One More Time," she was horrified. The record label's idea was for a cartoonish superhero theme, Britney knew she had to go for something edgier, something with attitude. Sitting on a plane, she came up with the idea of setting the video in the school. Everyone would wear school uniforms and sing and dance in the corridors and outside the school.

"She genuinely wanted to go down that road," says the video director, Nigel Dick. "It wasn't like we pushed Britney into doing anything. Most of the time you had to hold her back a bit."

It was also Britney who came up with the idea to tie her button-down shirt into a knot to reveal her midriff.

"The outfits looked kind of dorky, so I was like, 'Let's tie up our shirts and be cute,'" she explains. "It was about being a girl and knowing about fashion."

The video was shot at Rydell High School in California, where the movie *Grease* was filmed. It took two long days to get the video exactly right, but although it was hard work, everyone had plenty of time for goofing around in between takes, hanging out and making new friends.

The video was an immediate hit and gained heavy airplay on MTV's *Total Request Live* and Europe's *The Box*. Girls loved Britney's attitude and the way she dressed and the boys... well, they just loved Britney. The song itself couldn't fail to impress. From beginning to end it was so full of hooks that it just had to be a hit. From the minute it began with Britney's unforgettable, "Oh Baby, Baby," it leapt straight into your head and refused to leave.

As soon as "Baby, One More Time" appeared on the record store shelves, it began to sell almost as fast as the store assistants could stack it. There was no doubt about it Britney was big news. She was hot. You could hardly turn on the radio or MTV without hearing the song—it was always blaring out from somewhere. Released in November 1998, the single went straight to number 1. And just weeks after she turned 17 in December, her album did exactly the same. And not just in America, it seemed wherever the album was released it shot to the top of the charts. What a way to celebrate a birthday!

Although confident about her eventual success, Britney had no idea she'd be taking the world by storm so quickly. She was an international phenomenon. It was incredible... and also a little bit strange. The way it all exploded so quickly left her amazed, and more than a little bit dazed.

"The day they called me and said my album had debuted at number one I was so excited. I was like, 'Are you serious?' There are artists that are really, really big that never get to number one."

It had never happened like this before. And never to anyone so young. Britney is the first female and the youngest artist to simultaneously have the number one single on the *Billboard* 100 and the number one album on the *Billboard* 200 charts. Her album broke records by climbing the US charts higher and higher each week for five weeks...

"Baby, One More Time" hit the number 1 spot not only in the US, but in Canada, the UK, and Sweden, and made number 2 in Holland, Sweden, Norway, and Australia. In the UK it was the first record to spend more than a week at number 1 for eleven weeks and the record company had to press extra copies to meet the overwhelming demand. Britney had achieved worldwide recognition, something few artists ever manage to do. She'd broken records and was creating new ones almost as fast as anyone could stop and write them down.

It was obvious that Britney was an absolute, unstoppable, undeniable, certified smash.

It's been a little crazy. But I'm a little crazy

With the release of her next album, *Oops I Did It Again* Britney braced herself for a crazy ride. She knew the path ahead was going to be action-packed all the way and it has certainly lived up to her expectations. But there was an intense excitement as she embarked on a new chapter in her life.

One of the first things she wanted to do was take more control over her life. And who could blame her? When "Baby, One More Time" rocketed to the top of the charts, Britney was working every hour of the day and travelling to countries she didn't even know existed. She says now she didn't really like what she was going through.

"I was really confused and unhappy because I had no time for me," she explains. "And I wasn't enjoying the moment because I was stressing too much and feeling nervous about the future."

While Britney has always had a hand in selecting and writing her lyrics, designing her stage clothes and directing her videos, this year she stopped sharing a tour bus with her dancers and started setting some personal limits.

"In the beginning, everything was really cool, because it was so new to me," she says. "It's still exciting, but I find myself wanting to have a lot more time. I guess it's just me getting older and finding out more things about myself. So at night when I'm on the bus and putting on Macy Gray and lighting candles, it's my favourite time of day. Seriously."

It's no wonder, given her typical tour schedule. After an hour-and-a-half long concert comes a bus ride to the next town, a hotel bed around 3 am, a noon wake up call for press interviews and an autograph signing for fans.

She was and is still is very much aware that her first single was also the biggest of her career and that trying to beat that success was almost impossible. And her hectic schedule was starting to take its toll.

"Every day it was like, 'You have a meet and greet here, then we need you for an interview, then straight after that a TV show' and I just wanted to shout, 'No! I can't do this!' I got really caught up in it all, but it wasn't so much me as the people I worked for. So I decided to regain some control because I was feeling like a puppet. Now things are a lot smoother and I'm a lot happier because I can rely on my faith in God and realise that if my second album had only gone into the Top 30, so what? That's still a success. I can't expect to be No 1 all the time, can I!"

But it seems Britney certainly can. Her second album, *Oops I Did It Again*, did exactly what the title said. It shot into the charts at No 1 and sold an unprecedented 1.3 million copies in its first week of release.

And it's no wonder really because Britney has the sort of work ethic that leaves the rest of us breathless. Even being almost knocked out can't keep her down! While making the 'Oops' video, some stage equipment came loose and crashed down on Britney's head, leaving her needing four stitches. Did she take a week off to recuperate? Oh no. Not this girl. Britney, always the true professional, had a quick lie down and finished the video off by midnight. That's real dedication. But Britney's the kind of girl who is forever grateful for where she is and that's why she works so hard. And that's why she's still the darling of the pop world.

Britney's pop phenomenon shows no sign of disappearing. The singles, "Oops, I Did It Again", "Lucky", "Stronger" and "Don't Let Me Be The Last To Know" all shot to the top of the charts, ripping up the record books on their way. It seems everything Britney touches turns to gold and it isn't going to change. She's been signed up by Pepsi to star in their new campaign and she's even managed to find time to write a novel with her mum. Due to be published later in the year, it tells the story of a girl who is desperate to become a superstar. Something Britney definitely knows about!

One thing's for sure, Britney has enough talent to help her through whatever the future throws at her. The road ahead of her is endless. And Britney is happy to explore every opportunity.

Hanging Out with Britney

Fame has come quickly to Britney but she's taken to it like a natural. After all, she's been waiting for it all her life. Perhaps the most surprising thing about her success is that there's been absolutely no change in her. She's still the same home-loving, small-town, big-hearted Britney she's always been.

She's a professional. She knows that she's had good luck, but that only hard work will keep her at the top. And she's determined to be around for a long time to come. At heart, Britney's still the fan, the ordinary girl who's made it big. Fame hasn't gone to her head. She's still incredibly sane considering what the last few months have been like for her. Still, life as a celebrity can become overwhelming and it's sometimes very hard to hang on to yourself. Britney's success and fame came with a huge price tag. It might sound like a dream lifestyle—jetting all over the world, being adored by millions of people—but it can also be incredibly stressful. Britney hardly gets to see her family or friends, something she finds difficult to handle. But when it all gets too much, she simply heads back to the comfort of her home. And for Britney, that's very definitely where the heart is.

"When Britney gets homesick she'll just pop on a plane and come home," reveals her mom, Lynne. "The longest we've been apart is six weeks, which is hard, because she's still my little girl and I miss her."

Despite her huge success, Britney has remained remarkably normal. She says her heroes are her mom and dad and she still has her oldest friends with her all the way. Because she comes from such a close-knit town, where everybody knows everybody, her close friends are like sisters.

"They don't treat me any differently," she says. "If they kissed my butt, I'd kill them. Fake people, especially the kind of people who

say, 'Weren't you my friend two years ago?' I know who my real friends are because we grew up together back home. They haven't changed a bit and neither have I."

Like any other girl, Britney worries about pimples, bites her nails, and worries about running up huge phone bills, which is hard when you're away from home so much. She tries to stay in touch with her friends as much as possible when she's far away from her home-town. On the road she relies on text messages and her cell phone to catch up with her friends.

"It's really hard being away from them all so much," she sighs. "Because I have to travel such a lot I don't get to see them as much." So a mobile is essential for catching up with all the gossip.

Britney knows how important friendship is. She knows she can trust her friends always to be there for her to tell her the truth—whether or not she wants to hear it.

"My friends at home, know the real me, good and bad," she says. "It's always great to see them and catch up. We still fall out and argue, but we're still there for each other."

Britney enjoys her times at home when, for a brief time at least, she is out of the spotlight. She loves going to the cinema to catch a funny film or just hang-ing out with her friends, watching videos or TV and gossiping. She loves having the chance to shop till she drops, read romance novel after romance novel and

If they kissed my butt, I'd kill them

spend days at the beach. Yep, one thing's for certain: despite her huge fame, Britney's still as untar-nished as they come. One of her favorite days at home is Sunday, which is a real family day in the Spears household. The family go to church in the morning, then all gather in the family living room in the afternoon to eat Lynne's brownies and chat and watch TV.

Britney's mom is one of her best friends. Although she's very close to her dad, it's her mom she takes after the most. Britney says she's inherited her mother's weaknesses, such as biting her nails and wor-rying about every little thing she's said. Just like her other girlfriends, Britney knows she can count on her mom to be there for her, and often calls her from the road for advice.

Britney knows she's lucky to have such a close relationship with her mom. "I always have my mom to confide in," she says. "I think that's really important. There are a lot of my friends who never talk to their moms about anything. They have nobody to go to except their friends and if they're in the wrong crowd, who can they call on when they're in trouble?" She stresses she's no saint. "I've had my times when I've gone out and partied. I know what it's like. I don't want to do it again. Kids doing

drugs every weekend. It's because they're lacking something in their life—maybe the feeling of being loved."

Her mom calms Britney down when she's scared or feeling low, which is just one of the prices of fame. Her bodyguards and traveling staff do their best to make Britney as comfortable as possible but they can't always get rid of unwanted attention. Recently Britney was alone in her room in the Four Seasons hotel in LA. She was standing on the balcony and chatting with her mom on her cell phone, when she noticed an older man leering at her from a nearby balcony.

Oh God, Momma, I'm so scared

"The balconies were real close," she shudders, "And it freaked me out. I ran inside and I was like, 'Oh God, Momma, I'm so scared.'"

And as if that wasn't frightening enough, an uninvited young male fan recently showed up at the Spears family home demanding to meet with Britney. Now the singer's surrounded with bodyguards wherever she goes. They even hit the dancefloor with her when she goes clubbing, but even so she still has to deal with more than her fair share of drunken cretins.

"When I just want to dance and there's a lot of drunk guys standing there staring at me, it's like Ewwwwwww!" she admits. "I have to say the older fans are creepy. The forty-year-olds, people who are in your face too much. But Mom always tells me not to concern myself with them."

It's also Lynne who's kept Britney going when she's faced criticism during her career. The suggestive layout and cover that Britney did for *Rolling Stone* magazine sure got tongues wagging. Britney donned hot pants and vamped it up in her bedroom, prompting the Mississippi-based American Family Association, a media watchdog group, to launch a Britney boycott.

"When I saw the cover, I thought, 'Wow this is hot,' but I guess other people thought it was too sexy," says Britney. "I'm not going to walk around in hot pants and bra on the street, but when you're an artist you sometimes play a part. I'm a Christian, I go to church, but my mom taught us, 'Don't be ashamed of your body, it's a beautiful thing.'"

Whatever her critics thought, posing in revealing outfits was no big deal for Ms Spears. It was simply a case of Britney having fun, playing dress-up and experimenting with the way she looks. Something young girls do the world over.

"I was becoming a young woman," she says. "And it's nice to feel sexy sometimes."

Her good friend, Melissa Joan Hart, star of the hit show, *Sabrina The Teenage Witch*, also went

through a similar thing when she appeared in revealing outfits on two magazine covers, leading to a reprimand from *Sabrina*'s producers.

"We'd call each other and I'm like, 'God, how do you deal with this?'" says Melissa, who appeared in Britney's video "(You Drive Me) Crazy." "We both decided that we liked our decisions and we just had to stand by them."

Britney was hurt and surprised by the reaction to the photo-shoot.

"I knew I wasn't posing for a teen magazine. I felt good about what I did—and so did my parents, who were there during the shoot. I don't understand why it was made into such a big deal."

There were even suggestions that Jive Records was exploiting the young singer. After all, people were quick to whisper, what teenager could possibly achieve Britney's success without either being horribly ambitious or the result of pushy wannabe showbiz parents and record big-wigs? But her co-manager, Larry Rudolph, was quick to speak up.

"The record company wanted to keep things squeaky-clean and she went along with it at first," he says. "But it quickly became clear that this wasn't natural for her. She doesn't want anyone putting a blanket around her and [hiding] her, but she's totally in control of what's going on."

This wasn't the only criticism Britney's faced. Whispers about her fuller physique were becoming louder. Rumors began flying that she'd had breast implants. Britney finds the whole story incredible.

"Like I'm really going to get breast implants at seventeen?" she scoffs. She points out that she's a growing teenager and has gained about 15lb. Plus, like every most other teenage girls on the planet, she's very fond of push-up bras.
"Plastic surgery is a personal decision," Britney

The record company wanted to keep things squeaky-clean

says firmly, "And if women are doing it to make themselves feel better. I think it's fine. But sixteen, seventeen, eighteen is too young for surgery."

At first Britney thought the implant rumors were a joke. "Then I'd go up to people and they'd stare at my chest," she says. "And I was like, 'Eeeeewww!' But I had my cry and now I ignore it."

Like I'm really going to get breast implants at seventeen?

Britney's had to learn how to cope with the backlash to her fame, the "I Hate Britney" websites, the nasty rumors and the negative stories. The first thing she does after reading something bad about herself is pick up the phone and call her mom.

"I'll call her up, crying. I'll be devastated and she'll help me deal [with it]. It's so weird. Every week there's something in the tabloids. She's helped me just say, 'OK, whatever.' But there are days when I get down. Hormones, totally."

Her mother is very proud of the way Britney deals with the downside of her fame. She's always there to help her daughter through it, but has a tough job dealing with it herself.

"Britney handles it pretty well and she's gotten a tough skin on this. But I don't handle it so well. That's my baby they're telling lies about."

At the end of the day, Britney knows it's just a rumor, a silly story made up out of spite, or to sell papers, in the same way she's been accused of really being 28 years old. She now accepts that these stories are all part and parcel of her success.

"Now I try not to take any notice of it,' she states. "I wouldn't want to do anything else with my life, so the downside of being famous is not that bad."

The backlash has made Britney very aware of what it's like for teens who are constantly bombarded with unrealistic images. And it's something she wants to speak out about.

"Don't pay attention to what you read or see on TV. Just go with what you feel inside. Pay attention to you."

Britney and Boys

Britney was 14 when she started dating Reg Jones, the captain of the school football team. He was the school hunk and could have had any girl he wanted, but it was Britney who caught his eye. When he asked her out, she could hardly believe her luck. A romance, which many believed would end in wedding bells, started. Britney and Reg spent all their time together, going on holiday and enjoying days out riding, fishing, and white water rafting. Their relationship was loving, but not sexual. Britney is a devout Christian and has insisted she won't have sex until she gets married.

Britney told Reg all her hopes for her future as a singer and he encouraged her as she threw herself into the endless round of auditions and competitions. And he was one of the first people she rang when she got her record deal with Jive Records. But slowly the pressures of her fame and the differences in their lifestyles began to put a strain on their relationship. They both tried to keep things going. Reg ran up huge phone bills, as they spoke almost every day and night, but it was hard. Britney was busy flying around the world, recording her album and appearing on the radio. Reg's life carried on as normal in Kentwood and he found it difficult to adjust to hardly ever seeing Britney. Trying desperately to keep their romance alive, she poured out her feelings in letters to Reg. Even when she was away in Sweden recording the album that would change her life forever, she wrote to Reg begging him not to forget her. As her schedule became busier and busier, the relationship became harder and harder to maintain. But they loved each other dearly and were determined not to give up. Their relationship became a series of transatlantic phone calls and last-minute dashes up and down the country, snatching an hour together here and there. But it was hopeless. Britney's life had changed forever and deep down, both of them knew they were growing further and further apart. One night they sat down on the porch at Britney's parents' house and and talked everything through. They knew they had to split up. Through tears, hugs, and kisses they agreed to stay friends. Reg is still fiercely loyal to Britney and always speaks proudly about her. And they still talk regularly on the phone.

Britney insisted that she was far too busy to date anybody. Even if she had wanted to, it wasn't easy to meet boys. Most guys her age were a little intimidated by her fame, to say the least.

"Do you think they would come up to me at parties and chit chat?" asks Britney. "No, they didn't really say anything and acted really shy. But you know, I really didn't have time. I know that sounds selfish, but it would be more selfish if I tried and kept a boyfriend."

However, Britney has now found new love with N'Sync member Justin Timberlake. "I'm in love and I'm finally ready to admit it," she says. "We've been boyfriend and girlfriend for a long while now. And I guess I'd better start to talk about it, or else I'll be walking down the aisle before I admit to the world how much I love the guy."

The two of them have been friends for ever. They first met ten years ago while working together on Disney's New Mickey Mouse Club. From the very first moment Britney laid eyes on Justin she just knew she'd found someone very special.

Do you think they come up to me at parties and chit-chat?

"I think I fell in love with him way back then," she remembers. "I couldn't take my eyes off the guy."

And the couple are obviously head over heels in love. Britney just can't stop singing JuJu's—as she loves to call him—praises.

"I love his individuality," she smiles. "The fact he makes me laugh. Also he's incredibly sensitive and caring. He's just perfect."

It's no surprise Britney and Justin's feelings for each other run so deep, after all they're incredibly well suited. Almost as if they were meant to be. Both come from very loving, very close Baptist families and attribute their success to their rock-solid faith in God. They've both achieved world-wide fame in their teens, and they both share the same worries about the effects of such huge fame, managing their careers and growing away from their families. The pair have both agreed to put their families first, no matter what. And the two of them even have matching Mercedes! Britney's car is a sleek, white model, while Justin's is a racy red number. They also share the same taste in decor. When they're away on tour they both love making their trailers feel like home by filling them with lots of candles and burning incense. And they both agree that their mums' home cooking is the best in the world. They really are a match made in heaven.

Justin is very protective towards Britney and can give her all the support and understanding she needs. As a member of one of America's most popular boy bands he knows exactly what her life as a superstar is like and is able to help her deal with the stress and the strain that goes hand in hand with it. Just like Britney he's wanted to be famous for as long as he can remember. He loved performing from the moment he could talk and grabbed any opportunity to be in the spot light. At the tender age of ten he won a Dance Like New Kids On The Block talent contest and started having singing lessons. He knew straight away that singing was what he really wanted to do, so he and his friends started N' Sync. And the rest as they say is pop history.

Despite his incredible success Justin, like Britney, remains one of the nicest, most ordinary people in the world. Everyone who meets him can't help but be drawn to him. He's intelligent and kind and a real gentleman—the kind of guy who always holds the door open for a lady or happily gives up his seat on a train. No wonder Britney's fallen for him hook, line and sinker.

"He just makes me feel so grounded" is something she's often repeated in interviews with journalists. And it's not surprising. Justin, probably more than anyone she's ever met understands exactly what she goes through every day of her life. They both love music more than anything else in the world, but they are also very aware of the difficulty of balancing the hectic and very stressful lifestyle that comes with being

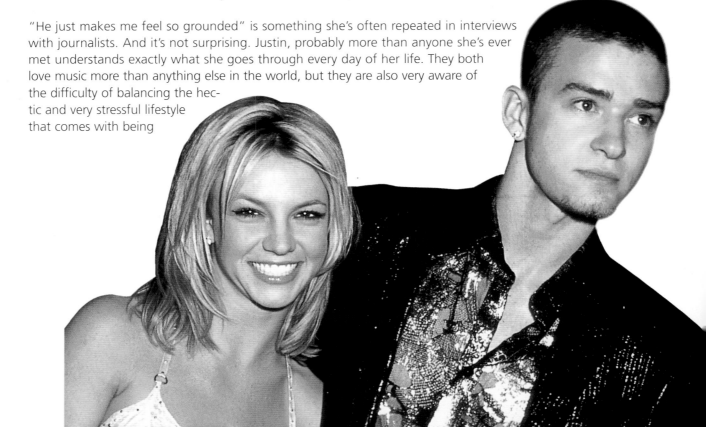

worldwide superstars. Especially when you're still in your teens. For Britney to have someone there who understands everything about her life, without her having to explain it is a dream come true. So it's no wonder she can no longer imagine her life without Justin by her side.

The pair are so in love that they've just bought a $2 million house in the very exclusive Beverly Hills area of LA. Britney and Justin spent more than a week in the Californian city looking for the perfect house together. It was hard work. They viewed house after house, but although each one was beautiful, none of them was quite right. But the minute they laid eyes on the stunning Mediterranean-style villa Britney knew that it was just what she'd been looking for—her dream house. It was absolutely perfect and Britney could hardly contain her excitement as she and Justin slowly wandered from room to room, exploring every little nook and cranny.

One of the things Britney loves the most is the fact it's so private. It's tucked away at the end of a very long private drive. There are four, very beautiful and very spacious bedrooms plus a guest house so the couple can have their families and friends staying whenever they want. And there's even a five car garage which is perfect for their Mercedes.

Britney and Justin were ready to sign on the dotted line, but first there were two other people's opinions they wanted to have. So both of them rang their mums and brought them out to give their all-important seal of approval, before the contract went ahead. Both of their mums fell in love with the house on sight and the deal was done.

Of course buying a house together has sparked off the usual tabloid rumours and speculation that it won't be long before the couple are walking down the aisle together. But Britney and Justin are both adamant that they are far too young for such a huge step. But Britney wants to make one thing clear—she is a virgin and so is Justin.

"We both plan to stay virgins until we get married," she insists, "It is tough to resist the temptation but we're both determined to keep ourselves pure until our wedding night. Justin and I are very lucky to have found each other. We share the same values and he totally understands that I have really strong morals. And just because I look sexy, it doesn't mean that I'm a naughty girl. I really believe true love waits!"

Britney and Clothes

Britney's influence is everywhere. If she wears a particular outfit on stage or to an awards ceremony, you can bet your bottom dollar that something similar will be flying off the shelves in stores all over the world in just a matter of weeks.

"She has an amazing sense of style and knows exactly what she wants," says stylist Sarah Parlow who worked with Britney during her European tour. "She has a great knowledge of the fashion world and always likes to support up-and-coming designers."

Britney's grown up a lot in the last year and her sense of style has followed suit.

"I change all the time," she laughs. "For a while I was really into Abercrombie & Fitch, because it's so comfy. But I've been getting a little more sophisticated. I'm wearing tighter jeans instead of those big pants all the time. I'm just totally into rock and roll style right now."

Britney is even responsible for the 'I'm wearing your T-shirt' craze that swept the planet. After seeing Britney wearing a Material Girl T-Shirt, Madonna gave Britney a bigger compliment than she could ever have dreamed possible and kick-started a whole new trend by having the words Britney Spears emblazoned across her chest on a little tee last autumn.

Britney is the kind of girl that most other girls can identify with. She just seems so normal, just like the girl next door. Her clothes, especially her beloved sweat pants, seem to have come straight off the racks of any department store. They're not even all that special, simply clothes that anyone would be happy wearing. Even the colors—pinks, whites, and blues—are ordinary. She's cute rather than beautiful, her hair is cut very simply but she always manages to look amazing without looking like she's tried too hard. With her graceful dancer's body and muscular physique, Britney likes clothes that show off her figure. She adores the street-inspired styles of Tommy Hilfiger, for whom she modeled in New York.

I'm getting a little more sophisticated...I'm into rock and roll style right now

Wherever I go—gas stations, Sunglass Hut—I'm always buying new shades

When it comes to make-up, Britney's favorite color is blue, but brown is her signature color for eye shadow and lip pencil. Her make-up bag is crammed with brand name products such as MAC, Face Stockholm, and Shu Uemura. And shimmering powders are an absolute essential when it comes to showing off Britney's smooth skin under the hot spotlights.

Because of her hectic lifestyle, Britney tries to look after her diet. She eats whatever she wants to, but tries to stick to healthy foods such as fresh vegetables and plenty of fruit. She also makes sure she drinks plenty of water, at least three litres a day.

However, like most teenagers, she adores junk food.

"Ooh, I love bad food," she smiles. "Like a chicken sandwich with cheese from Burger King. It's like the best. And greasy French fries. And a Coke. That just makes me feel so much better. So bad for you, but so good."

Recently though, Britney has been tweaking her image. She got her navel pierced and now wears a silver and turquoise belly ring. She's also got a tattoo. She has a small black-winged fairy that peeks out of the top of her hipsters and jogging pants. Britney had been dying to get a tattoo after a Christmas trip to Hawaii with her friends. When she returned to New York her hair stylist recommended a tattoo artist in the Garment District. As soon as she could

Ooh, I love bad food," she smiles. "Like a chicken sandwich with cheese from Burger King. It's like the best. And greasy French fries. And a Coke. That just makes me feel so much better. So bad for you, but so good

Britney went to the tattoo studio, accompanied by her bodyguard and her chaperone, and immediately picked out the little fairy. It was inked carefully on to the bottom of her spine. "And it really, really hurt," says Britney, but she loves it.

Despite her young age, Britney totally understands the music business. She knows she is working in an extremely fickle industry and is determined to stay one step ahead. One thing's for certain though, whether she's in sweat pants or a Chloe jumpsuit, Britney always looks a billion dollars. And just because she looks and dresses like a girl, loves make-up, and obsesses about clothes it would be a major mistake not to take her seriously. There's an awful lot going on with this little lady. And just because she looks like a living doll, it doesn't mean she can't pack a punch as well.

the FUTURE

Britney's star shows no sign of fading. Her schedule for the next year and a half is mapped out.

She's starring in her very first Hollywood movie. Although she has made guest appearances on TV shows like *Sabrina The Teenage Witch* alongside one of her very best friends, Melissa Joan Hart, *Going On The Road* is her first big-screen role.

Britney plays Lucy, a school swot who goes on a road trip across California with two of her wild, childhood friends Kit and Mini. The film makers were determined to make the most of her talents and made sure there was also a lot of music along the way. The three girls meet an aspiring musician who persuades them to go with him to Los Angeles to take part in a musical contest. The musician also plays Britney's love interest and the pair had to share a tender kiss in a restaurant. Britney says she closed her eyes and thought of Justin. It certainly worked because she manages to look very much in love!

Much of the filming has taken place in Britney's home town of Louisiana and large crowds gathered every

Right now the future's so bright Britney must be pinching herself on a regular basis to make sure she's not dreaming. She has broken out of any mould that could have cramped.or altered her and become a bigger sensation because of it. Her second album showed how much she had developed as an artist since her debut album, and her third promises to take her to another level. Britney's now that little bit wiser, far more confident, and completely in control of her own career.

41

I don't want to be a singer who sings a song just to sing

day, desperate to catch even the tiniest glimpse of the local girl. Although she was very nervous about acting, Britney made sure that, however busy she was, she always made time to smile and wave at her fans and stopped to chat with them whenever she could find an opportunity.

Britney's taken to acting as if she'd been doing it all her life, although it's not always easy. *Going On The Road* calls for her to break down three times, not easy for someone as naturally happy as Britney. But unlike many other actresses who just reach for a tear stick, she was determined to do it properly. She learnt how to reach inside herself for some of the sadder times in her life to make herself cry.

"You're gonna think I'm crazy," she laughs, "But we all have inner demons, things that make us upset. I just picture them and put them in my throat." She uses a different one every time, pretending that she's stressed out or that she misses her mum.

Britney is forever pushing herself further and further. She loves the challenge of acting and the fact that it allows her to explore even more of her creativity. But her heart lies in singing and that will always be the most important thing to her, no matter where else her career may take her.

"I want music always to be part of my life," she says. "Music will always be my main priority. Just like Madonna. I respect her so much because she keeps changing her music and image to stay fresh."

Britney is determined her third album will outdo the success of the last two and is planning to make her stage shows even more spectacular. Her talent, foresight and refusal to compromise has inspired hundreds of budding young singers who have realised there is still room for people dedicated to producing good pop music.

She's had to fight to get her success, but now she's got it, she's enjoying it and millions of record-buying fans are enjoying it right alongside her. Britney's shown the world how with determination, the right intentions and self-belief, it's possible to overcome pretty much anything to achieve your dreams.

I want music always to be part of my life...Music will always be my main priority

It's no wonder she's has won almost every award going. She's already worth an estimated $10 million. And all this before she even hit twenty! Not bad for an ordinary girl from Louisiana. Her meteoric rise to international fame has been a combination of serious talent, hard work and the vision of a girl who dared to dream.

The truth is Britney Spears appeals to absolutely everybody. Girls want to be her, boys want to kiss her and the most famous woman in pop wants to wear her t-shirt! The Queen of Teen has finally come of age. It's one hundred percent cool to dig Britney. It's official.

She's worked incredibly hard to get where she is. And through it all she's remained a pleasant, grounded girl who loves life and gives everyone a chance, no matter who they are. There's not a lot of that around in the music business.

She's learnt a lot, met all kinds of interesting people and achieved the kind of success that she could never have imagined even in her wildest dreams. And one thing's for sure, we ain't seen nothing yet.

Britney's having the trip of a lifetime and nothing could possibly stop it.

I'd like to put a little dance into everyone's life

Britney test your knowledge

Ok, so now you've read the Britney story, it's time to check how much you really know about the singer.

1. How old was Britney when she joined the Mickey Mouse Club?
a) Eleven
b) Eight
c) Fourteen

2. Where did Britney record her first album?
a) Scotland
b) Sweden
c) South Africa

3. Which is Britney's favorite clothes label?
a) Bebe
b) Tommy Hilfiger
c) Calvin Klein

4. What's Britney's big brother called?
a) Bryan
b) Benjy
c) Bill

5. Which record company is Britney signed to?
a) Jazz Records
b) Jive Records
c) Jiff Records

6. What movie was filmed at the same school as Britney's "Baby One More Time" video?
a) *My Best Friend's Wedding*
b) *Steel Magnolias*
c) *Grease*

7. What does Britney have a tattoo of?
a) A rose
b) A fairy
c) The Chinese sign for peace

8. Which band did Britney tour with as their opening act?
a) The Backstreet Boys
b) 'NSync
c) N Tyce

9. What was the last name of Britney's last boyfriend?
a) Jones
b) Smith
c) Roberts

10. Who did Britney have lunch with in a Planet Hollywood restaurant?
a) Justin Timberlake
b) Nick Carter
c) Ben Affleck

11. How many awards did Britney manage to nab at MTV Europe Music Awards?
a) Four
b) Ten
c) Six

12. What was the name of the broadway show Britney starred in when she was eleven?
a) Cats
b) Closer
c) Ruthless

13. A feature in which magazine caused the Mississippi-based American Family Association to launch a Britney boycott?
a) Rolling Stone
b) Vogue
c) Esquire

14. What's Britney's favorite color?
a) Black
b) Baby blue
c) Red

15. What does Britney collect?
a) Shells
b) Stamps
c) Angels

16. What was the name of Britney's high school?
a) Parklane Academy
b) Springfield High
c) Highbury High

17. What is Britney's favorite junk food?
a) Chicken sandwich with cheese from Burger King
b) Chicken pizza with extra toppings from Pizza Hut
c) Chicken wings and fries from Kentucky Fried Chicken

18. What was the first idea for Britney's "Baby, One More Time" Video?
a) A futuristic, space-type scenario
b) A cartoonish superhero theme
c) A schoolgirl motif

19. Who wrote Britney's single "Sometimes"?
a) Dianne Warren
b) Lionel Ritchie
c) Nick Carter

20. Whose long career does Britney hope to emulate?
a) The Beatles
b) Elvis
c) Madonna

Answers
Check out your answers here

1) a	8) b	15) c
2) b	9) a	16) a
3) all three	10) c	17) a
4) a	11) a	18) b
5) b	12) c	19) a
6) c	13) a	20) c
7) b	14) b	

Conclusions—so how well did you do?

Baby, One More Time
0–8
Oh dear, are you sure you didn't mean to pick up a book on Christina Aguilera instead? Or did you just buy this book for the gorgeous pictures of the girl herself? Put "Oops I Did It Again" on the stereo, whack up the volume, turn to the beginning of this book, and start reading it all over again. And make sure you pay attention this time. Oh, and repeat, "Britney rocks" ten times before you go to bed.

Sometimes
9–15
Hmm, not a bad score but you could do better. You like the songs and you know Britney's middle name, but it's the little details that make up the whole picture, you know. You can't call yourself a true fan unless you know everything from what Britney likes for breakfast to what time she goes to bed at night. Try repeating "I will learn everything there is to know about Britney" five times every morning before you get up.

Oops I Did It Again
16–20
You are a true blue Britney fan. You know all her songs by heart, where she lives, and even the names of her childhood friends. Give yourself a pat on the back and rest assured in the knowledge that Britney would probably be only too proud to introduce you to her mother. Well done you!

Getting in touch with *Britney*

Getting in touch with Britney isn't difficult. If you have access to a computer she can be reached at:

www.britneyspears.com

There are now literally thousands of other Britney Spears sites on the World Wide Web.

To start you off, here are some of the better sites around.

The official Britney site is at www.officialbritney.com

The other sites are all unofficial, but that doesn't mean they're not as good. All of the following contain plenty of pictures and information. Some have great audio and video clips as well:

babetopbritneyspear.tripod.com/home.html

wallofsound.go.com/artists/britneyspears/home.html

Before you log off make sure you check out the famous Society of the Future Husbands Of Britney Spears site. It can be found at: www.sfhbs.com

And, of course, there are more appearing every day.